Badlands
National Park

by Grace Hansen

NATIONAL PARKS

Abdo Kids Jumbo is an Imprint of Abdo Kids
abdobooks.com

abdobooks.com

Published by Abdo Kids, a division of ABDO, P.O. Box 398166, Minneapolis, Minnesota 55439.
Copyright © 2019 by Abdo Consulting Group, Inc. International copyrights reserved in all countries.
No part of this book may be reproduced in any form without written permission from the publisher.
Abdo Kids Jumbo™ is a trademark and logo of Abdo Kids.

102018

012019

Photo Credits: Alamy, iStock, Shutterstock, ©Sharon Mollerus p.19/CC-BY-2.0

Production Contributors: Teddy Borth, Jennie Forsberg, Grace Hansen

Design Contributors: Dorothy Toth, Laura Mitchell

Library of Congress Control Number: 2018945978

Publisher's Cataloging-in-Publication Data

Names: Hansen, Grace, author.

Title: Badlands National Park / by Grace Hansen.

Description: Minneapolis, Minnesota : Abdo Kids, 2019 | Series: National parks
    Includes glossary, index and online resources (page 24).

Identifiers: ISBN 9781532182068 (lib. bdg.) | ISBN 9781532183041 (ebook) |
    ISBN 9781532183539 (Read-to-me ebook)

Subjects: LCSH: Badlands National Park (S.D.)--Juvenile literature. | National
    parks and reserves--Juvenile literature. | Badlands National Monument (S.D.)--
    Juvenile literature. | Badlands--Juvenile literature.

Classification: DDC 978.3--dc23

Table of Contents

Badlands National Park

Badlands National Park is in South Dakota. It was made a national monument in 1939. It wasn't until 1978 that it became a national park.

4

5

Climate

The park's **climate** is extreme. It can be very hot or cold. It can flood with rain. **Droughts** can cause fires.

7

Nature & Natural Features

Badlands animals are tough.

They have **adapted** to the

park's living conditions.

Gopher snakes and racers are common reptiles in the Badlands. They sleep during the long, cold winters. They might even share dens.

Big bison roam the grassy prairies. Tiny prairie dogs live among them. The rodents' underground homes keep them safe.

Western wheatgrass rules the park's prairies. It grows one to two feet (.3-.6 m) high.

15

Other **native** grasses, like
prairie coneflower, grow too.
The grasses are an important
food source for the animals.

17

The land changes from grasslands to high rock formations. The large, pointed rocks are called pinnacles. Bighorn sheep can be spotted on even the steepest rocks.

The Stronghold Unit of the park is part of the Pine Ridge Indian Reservation. Members of the **Oglala Lakota Tribe** own the land. They manage and protect it.

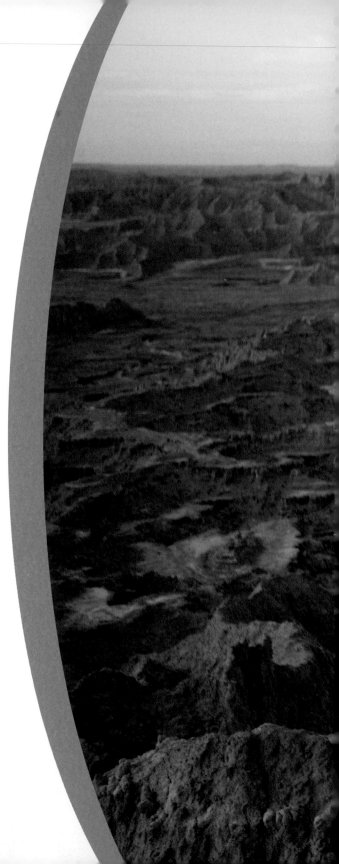

Fun Activities

Bike Badlands Loop Road

Gaze at more than 7,500 visible stars and the Milky Way Galaxy at night

Hike one of the many trails

View fossils found in the park in the Paleontology Lab

Glossary

adapt – to change for a particular use or become used to.

climate – the usual weather in a place.

drought – a long period with little to no rain.

native – original to.

Oglala Lakota Tribe – a group of Native Americans and one of the seven subtribes of the Lakota people. The Lakota live in North and South Dakota.

paleontology – the science that studies animal and plant fossils for information about life in the past.

reptile – a cold-blooded animal with a skeleton inside its body and dry scales or hard plates on its skin.

23

Index

Abdo Kids
ONLINE
FREE! ONLINE MULTIMEDIA RESOURCES

Visit **abdokids.com** and
use this code to access crafts,
games, videos, and more!

Abdo Kids Code:
NBK2068

24